Jack K,

the new
choice

Primary
Dictionary

THE PRIMARY DICTIONARY – AT A GLANCE

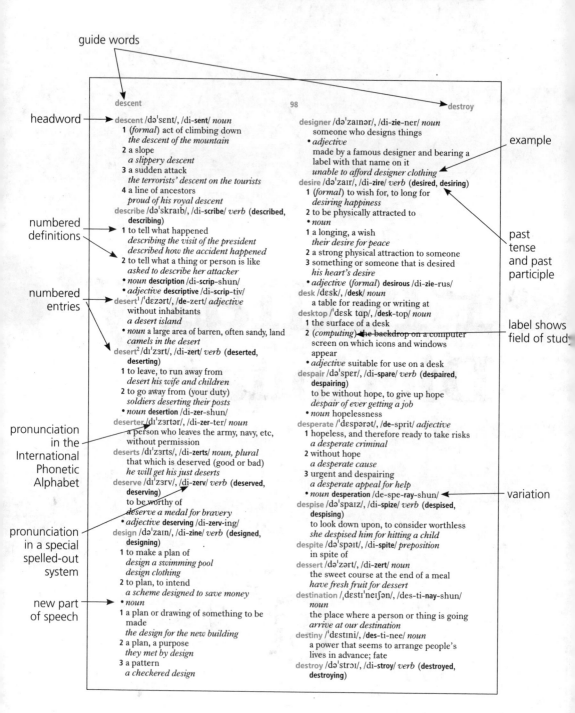

guide words

headword

numbered
definitions

numbered
entries

pronunciation
in the
International
Phonetic
Alphabet

pronunciation
in a special
spelled-out
system

new part
of speech

example

past
tense
and past
participle

label shows
field of study

variation

descent /dəˈsɛnt/, /di-**sent**/ *noun*
  1 (*formal*) act of climbing down
    the descent of the mountain
  2 a slope
    a slippery descent
  3 a sudden attack
    the terrorists' descent on the tourists
  4 a line of ancestors
    proud of his royal descent
describe /dəˈskraɪb/, /di-**scribe**/ *verb* (**described,
  describing**)
  1 to tell what happened
    describing the visit of the president
    described how the accident happened
  2 to tell what a thing or person is like
    asked to describe her attacker
  • *noun* **description** /di-**scrip**-shun/
  • *adjective* **descriptive** /di-**scrip**-tiv/
desert[1] /ˈdɛzərt/, /**de**-zert/ *adjective*
  without inhabitants
  a desert island
  • *noun* a large area of barren, often sandy, land
    camels in the desert
desert[2] /dɪˈzɜrt/, /di-**zert**/ *verb* (**deserted,
  deserting**)
  1 to leave, to run away from
    desert his wife and children
  2 to go away from (your duty)
    soldiers deserting their posts
  • *noun* **desertion** /di-**zer**-shun/
deserter /dɪˈzɜrtər/, /di-**zer**-ter/ *noun*
  a person who leaves the army, navy, etc,
  without permission
deserts /dɪˈzɜrts/, /di-**zerts**/ *noun, plural*
  that which is deserved (good or bad)
  he will get his just deserts
deserve /dɪˈzɜrv/, /di-**zerv**/ *verb* (**deserved,
  deserving**)
  to be worthy of
  deserve a medal for bravery
  • *adjective* **deserving** /di-**zerv**-ing/
design /dəˈzaɪn/, /di-**zine**/ *verb* (**designed,
  designing**)
  1 to make a plan of
    design a swimming pool
    design clothing
  2 to plan, to intend
    a scheme designed to save money
  • *noun*
  1 a plan or drawing of something to be
    made
    the design for the new building
  2 a plan, a purpose
    they met by design
  3 a pattern
    a checkered design

designer /dəˈzaɪnər/, /di-**zie**-ner/ *noun*
  someone who designs things
  • *adjective*
  made by a famous designer and bearing a
  label with that name on it
  unable to afford designer clothing
desire /dəˈzaɪr/, /di-**zire**/ *verb* (**desired, desiring**)
  1 (*formal*) to wish for, to long for
    desiring happiness
  2 to be physically attracted to
  • *noun*
  1 a longing, a wish
    their desire for peace
  2 a strong physical attraction to someone
  3 something or someone that is desired
    his heart's desire
  • *adjective* (*formal*) **desirous** /di-**zie**-rus/
desk /dɛsk/, /**desk**/ *noun*
  a table for reading or writing at
desktop /ˈdɛsk tɑp/, /**desk**-top/ *noun*
  1 the surface of a desk
  2 (*computing*) the backdrop on a computer
    screen on which icons and windows
    appear
  • *adjective* suitable for use on a desk
despair /dəˈspɛr/, /di-**spare**/ *verb* (**despaired,
  despairing**)
  to be without hope, to give up hope
  despair of ever getting a job
  • *noun* **hopelessness**
desperate /ˈdɛspərət/, /**de**-sprit/ *adjective*
  1 hopeless, and therefore ready to take risks
    a desperate criminal
  2 without hope
    a desperate cause
  3 urgent and despairing
    a desperate appeal for help
  • *noun* **desperation** /de-spe-**ray**-shun/
despise /dəˈspaɪz/, /di-**spize**/ *verb* (**despised,
  despising**)
  to look down upon, to consider worthless
  she despised him for hitting a child
despite /dəˈspaɪt/, /di-**spite**/ *preposition*
  in spite of
dessert /dəˈzɜrt/, /di-**zert**/ *noun*
  the sweet course at the end of a meal
  have fresh fruit for dessert
destination /ˌdɛstɪˈneɪʃən/, /des-ti-**nay**-shun/
  noun
  the place where a person or thing is going
  arrive at our destination
destiny /ˈdɛstɪni/, /**des**-ti-nee/ *noun*
  a power that seems to arrange people's
  lives in advance; fate
destroy /dəˈstrɔɪ/, /di-**stroy**/ *verb* (**destroyed,
  destroying**)

THE PRIMARY DICTIONARY – AT A GLANCE

guide words

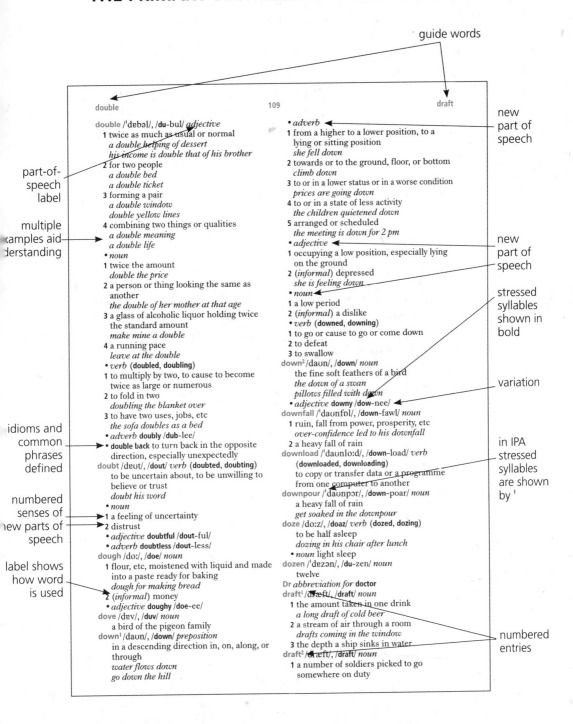

part-of-speech label

multiple examples aid understanding

idioms and common phrases defined

numbered senses of new parts of speech

label shows how word is used

new part of speech

new part of speech

stressed syllables shown in bold

variation

in IPA stressed syllables are shown by '

numbered entries

double /'dɐbəl/, /du-bul/ *adjective*
1 twice as much as usual or normal
a double helping of dessert
his income is double that of his brother
2 for two people
a double bed
a double ticket
3 forming a pair
a double window
double yellow lines
4 combining two things or qualities
a double meaning
a double life
• *noun*
1 twice the amount
double the price
2 a person or thing looking the same as another
the double of her mother at that age
3 a glass of alcoholic liquor holding twice the standard amount
make mine a double
4 a running pace
leave at the double
• *verb* (**doubled, doubling**)
1 to multiply by two, to cause to become twice as large or numerous
2 to fold in two
doubling the blanket over
3 to have two uses, jobs, etc
the sofa doubles as a bed
• *adverb* doubly /dub-lee/
• **double back** to turn back in the opposite direction, especially unexpectedly

doubt /dɐʊt/, /dout/ *verb* (**doubted, doubting**)
to be uncertain about, to be unwilling to believe or trust
doubt his word
• *noun*
1 a feeling of uncertainty
2 distrust
• *adjective* doubtful /dout-ful/
• *adverb* doubtless /dout-less/

dough /doʊ/, /doe/ *noun*
1 flour, etc, moistened with liquid and made into a paste ready for baking
dough for making bread
2 (*informal*) money
• *adjective* doughy /doe-ee/

dove /dɐv/, /duv/ *noun*
a bird of the pigeon family

down¹ /daʊn/, /down/ *preposition*
in a descending direction in, on, along, or through
water flows down
go down the hill

• *adverb*
1 from a higher to a lower position, to a lying or sitting position
she fell down
2 towards or to the ground, floor, or bottom
climb down
3 to or in a lower status or in a worse condition
prices are going down
4 to or in a state of less activity
the children quietened down
5 arranged or scheduled
the meeting is down for 2 pm
• *adjective*
1 occupying a low position, especially lying on the ground
2 (*informal*) depressed
she is feeling down
• *noun*
1 a low period
2 (*informal*) a dislike
• *verb* (**downed, downing**)
1 to go or cause to go or come down
2 to defeat
3 to swallow

down² /daʊn/, /down/ *noun*
the fine soft feathers of a bird
the down of a swan
pillows filled with down
• *adjective* downy /dow-nee/

downfall /'daʊnfɔːl/, /down-fawl/ *noun*
1 ruin, fall from power, prosperity, etc
over-confidence led to his downfall
2 a heavy fall of rain

download /'daʊnloʊd/, /down-load/ *verb*
(**downloaded, downloading**)
to copy or transfer data or a programme from one computer to another

downpour /'daʊnpɔːr/, /down-poar/ *noun*
a heavy fall of rain
get soaked in the downpour

doze /doʊz/, /doaz/ *verb* (**dozed, dozing**)
to be half asleep
dozing in his chair after lunch
• *noun* light sleep

dozen /'dɐzən/, /du-zen/ *noun*
twelve

Dr *abbreviation for* **doctor**

draft¹ /drɑːft/, /draft/ *noun*
1 the amount taken in one drink
a long draft of cold beer
2 a stream of air through a room
drafts coming in the window
3 the depth a ship sinks in water

draft² /drɑːft/, /draft/ *noun*
1 a number of soldiers picked to go somewhere on duty

A GUIDE TO THE DICTIONARY

A dictionary is a useful tool to help you find the spelling, meaning and pronunciation of a word, quickly and easily. It will also help you to be confident and sure about using words correctly when speaking and writing. This modern dictionary, with simple definitions for younger readers, provides over 8,000 concise, up-to-date dictionary definitions. A specially commissioned, crystal-clear pronunciation guide and a clear, modern layout creates a book that is accessible for everyone.

Headword

The **headword** is what we call the word in bold at the beginning of each entry in a dictionary. This is the word that is being explained in the **definition** (see below). The headword is set out further in the margin than the other parts of the entry so it is easy to find. The words indicated below by arrow are headwords.

> ⟶ **a** /ə, eɪ/, /a/ *indefinite article* (**an** /æn/, /an/ before a vowel)
> ⟶ **aardvark** /ˈɑrdvɑrk/, /**ard**-vark/ *noun*
> ⟶ **abandon** /əˈbændən/, /a-**ban**-don/ *verb* (**abandoned, abandoning**)
> ⟶ **abandoned** /əˈbændənd/, /a-**ban**-dond/ *adjective*
> ⟶ **abbreviate** /əˈbriːvɪˌeɪt/, /a-**bree**-vee-ate/ *verb* (**abbreviated, abbreviating**)

Definition

Definition is the name for the meaning of a word. The area indicated by an arrow below shows the definition of "**avocado**".

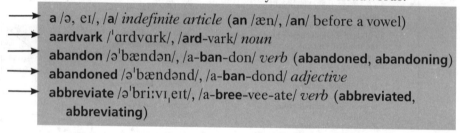

> **avocado** /ˌævəˈkɒdoː/, /a-ve-**ka**-do/ *noun*
> definition ⟶ a pear-shaped fruit with a hard, dark green skin, soft, pale green flesh, and a large stone, used in salads, etc

Numbered senses

Sometimes a word can have several different meanings when used in different ways. In this book these new meanings are numbered and given a new line, as you can see in the shaded box below.

> **bank** /bæŋk/, /**bangk**/ *noun*
> definition 1 ⟶ **1** a ridge or mound of earth, etc
> definition 2 ⟶ **2** the ground at the side of a river, lake, etc
> definition 3 ⟶ **3** a place where money is put for safekeeping

Numbered entries

Words of **different origins** and different definitions, but with the same spelling, are given separate, numbered entries.

numbered entries indicated with a superscript number

case[1] /keɪs/, /**case**/ *noun*

1 a box or container
a watch in a case

2 a covering
seed cases of plants

3 a suitcase
my holiday case is packed

4 a piece of furniture for displaying or containing things
a glass case in the jewellery shop

case[2] /keɪs/, /**case**/ *noun*

1 an event, instance, or example
a case of measles

2 a person having medical, etc, treatment
a psychiatric case

3 a statement of facts and arguments or reasons
there's a good case for believing him

Alphabetical order

The headwords in this book are listed in **alphabetical order**, that means they follow the order of the letters that appear in the alphabet from A through to Z.

If the first letter of both words is the same then the words are ordered by the second letter: **mature** comes before **meadow**. If the second letters are also the same then look at the third letter: **abandon** comes before **abbey**, and so on. Here are some words beginning with "**bar**", shown in order:

bar /bɑr/, /**bar**/ *noun*
barb /bɑrb/, /**barb**/ *noun*
barber /bɑrbər/, /**bar**-ber/ *noun*
bar code /ˈbɑrkoːd/, /**bar**-code/ *noun*
bare /bɛr/, /**bare**/ *adjective*

Pronunciation

Pronunciation is how words sound when they are spoken. There are pronunciation guides for all the headwords in our book. There are two guides, one showing phonetic symbols, and one with "spelled-out" guides that use combinations of letters to describe the sounds as simply as possible. Both pronunciation guides appear right after the headword like this: **difficult** /ˈdɪfɪˌkəlt/, /**di**-fi-cult/, with IPA first and the spelled-out guide second. Say out loud the words in bold that follow:

answer, canoe, fruit, ghost, gnu, phone

This is how we describe their pronunciation in this book:

answer /ˈænsər/, /**an**-ser/	**canoe** /kəˈnuː/, /ca-**noo**/
ghost /ɡoːst/, /**goast**/	**fruit** /fruːt/, /**froot**/
gnu /nuː/, /**noo**/	**phone** /foːn/, /**foan**/

For those familiar with IPA there is also a phonetic guide. Below is a key to the phonetic symbols used in the book.

Vowels

æ	hat, saddle, baggy
ɑ	ajar, alarm, apart
əɪ	bile, bike, alight
aɪ	high, hive, strive
aʊ	shout, bough, couch
ɛ	fret, vet, says, said
eɪ	way, hey, cage, neigh
ɪ	hit, sieve, kitty, build, women
iː	heave, jeep, siege
ɒ	hot, got, allotment, bother
ɔː	thought, fraught, thaw
oː	note, float, tote, boat
ɔɪ	boy, avoid, employ
ʊ	woman, wood, could
ɐ	trump, front, flood
uː	true, brew, you, shoe
ə	the, harder, doctor, brewer

Consonants

The following consonant symbols have the usual meaning b, d, f, h, k, l, m, n, p, r, s, t, v, w, z

ɡ	ghost, example [ɛɡˈzæmpl], give
j	yes, senior [sinjər], onion [ɐnjən], future [fjuːtʃər]
ʃ	should, machine, sugar
ʒ	leisure, azure, invasion
tʃ	hatch, capture, chew
dʒ	jam, hedge [hɛdʒ], soldier [səʊldʒər]
θ	thin, breath, thoughts
ð	there, then, the, breathe
ŋ	sing, linger [lɪŋɡər], amazing
f	cough, enough, fan
k	box [bɒks], cart, hike
x	loch [the Scots voiceless uvular fricative sound]

Syllables and stresses

Words are made up of syllables. These are the different blocks of sound within the word. For the spelled-out pronunciations in this book, the syllables are divided by hyphens (-). Each word has a stressed syllable. The word "**apologize**" has four syllables and the stressed one is the sound "**pol**". Spelled-out stressed syllables are marked in bold, and in IPA they have a ' symbol in front of them. The word "**gymnasium**" has four syllables too, and the syllable that is stressed is the sound "**nay**".

apologize /əˈpɒləˌdʒaɪz/, /a-**pol**-o-jize/
gymnasium /dʒɪmˈneɪziəm/, /jim-**nay**-zee-um/

Variations of spelling

Sometimes words can be spelled in two or more equally acceptable ways. For example, a lot of words that end in **-ise** can also be spelled with **-ize** instead. **Colour** is a British English spelling, and **color** is the American English spelling. Variations are in bold type at the end of the line that contains the headword.

> **nationalize** /ˈnæʃnəˌlaɪz/, /**nash**-na-lize/ *verb, also* **nationalise**
> **organize** /**awr**-ga-nize/ *verb, also* **organise**
> **practise** /**prac**-tiss/ *verb* (*British*), *also* **practice** (*US*)
> **programme** /**pro**-gram/ *noun, also* **program** (*US*)
> **realize** /**ree**-a-lize/ *verb, also* **realise**

Parts of speech

In this book you will see words in italic type following the headword and pronunciation.

part of
speech
label
appears
in italic
type

> **doll** /dɒl/, /**dol**/ *noun*
>   a toy in the shape of a person
>   *a baby doll*

These words tell us what **part of speech** the headword is. That is, what **function** the word has in English. Is the word the name of a thing (**noun**)? Does the word name an action (**verb**)? Does the word describe a thing (**adjective**)? Does the word describe what an action was like (**adverb**)? Does it refer to the position of a thing (**preposition**)?

Dictionary entries with more than one part of speech

Some words can function as several different parts of speech, depending on their use, and you will see examples in the dictionary indicated with a • within an entry.

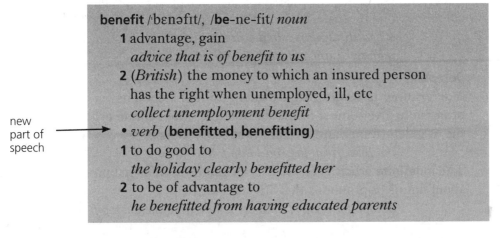

> **benefit** /ˈbɛnəfɪt/, /**be**-ne-fit/ *noun*
>   **1** advantage, gain
>   *advice that is of benefit to us*
>   **2** (*British*) the money to which an insured person
>   has the right when unemployed, ill, etc
>   *collect unemployment benefit*
>   • *verb* (**benefitted, benefitting**)
>   **1** to do good to
>   *the holiday clearly benefitted her*
>   **2** to be of advantage to
>   *he benefitted from having educated parents*

new
part of
speech

Noun

A noun is used to refer to a person, thing or quality. It is sometimes referred to as "**a naming word**".

A **common noun** refers to something of which there are many examples, words like **boy**, **bread**, **coin**, **tiger**, **tree**. Nouns can refer to concepts and ideas as well as things that you can touch: **honesty**, **love**, **rebellion**, **science**, **trust**, **hope**.

A **proper noun** is often a name. It refers to something of which there is only one example. Proper nouns begin with a **capital letter**. Examples are: **France**, **French**, **Antarctica**, **Elizabeth**, **the Pope**.

A **plural** refers to more than one thing. With nouns this is usually shown by adding an "**-s**", "**-es**", or "**-ies**" (after y) to the end of a noun, but some words break this rule. These are **irregular plurals** such as: **women**, **men**, **children**, **oxen**, **die** (plural of dice), **media**. In the dictionary these irregular plurals appear in bold, within brackets, following the part of speech.

> **man** /mæn/, /**man**/ *noun* (*plural* **men** /mɛn/, /**men**/)
> **yourself** /jɔr‚sɛlf/, /yoor-**self**/ *pronoun* (*plural* **yourselves** /jɔr'sɛlvz/, /**yoor**-selvz/)

Pronoun

A pronoun is a word that takes the place of a noun or noun phrase in a sentence. Examples are: **I**, **we**, **you**, **he**, **she**, **it**, **they**, **him**, **her** and **them**.

Adjective

An adjective is a word that describes or gives more information about **nouns** or **pronouns**. Adjectives usually tell us something about the colour, size, quantity, quality or classification. Examples are **nice**, **suitable**, **good**, **bad**, **red**, **blue**, **dangerous**.

If you use more than one adjective then the order is important: general opinion, specific opinion, size, shape, age, colour, nationality, material.

> *a beautiful, varnished oak door*
> *a ghastly, uncomfortable, yellow dress*

Determiner

A determiner is a word that is used in front of a noun or pronoun to give some information about it. The **definite article**, **the**, is a determiner and it refers to specific things.

> *the first train, the road into town*

The **indefinite article** is either **a** or **an** and gives information about nouns or pronouns that are not specific.

> *a hope for a cure, a lovely smell, an expensive gift*

Other examples of determiners include: **this, that, these** and **those**; **all, any, both, each, either, every, few, little, less, many, much, more, neither, no, several, some** and **neither**; and **numbers** are sometimes classified as determiners.

Verb

The verb is the word in a sentence that is most concerned with the action – a **doing word** – and without it you cannot make an acceptable sentence. Verb endings change according to how they are used, this is called **inflection**, and this shows **tense** and whether the action is by one person or more. In this book we show **past tense** and **past and present participles** (**regular** and **irregular** forms) in bold, within brackets, following the part of speech:

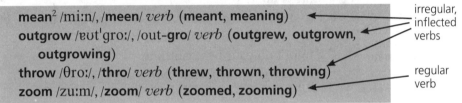

mean[2] /miːn/, /**meen**/ *verb* (**meant, meaning**) ← irregular, inflected verbs
outgrow /ɐʊtˈɡroː/, /out-**gro**/ *verb* (**outgrew, outgrown, outgrowing**) ←
throw /θroː/, /**thro**/ *verb* (**threw, thrown, throwing**) ←
zoom /zuːm/, /**zoom**/ *verb* (**zoomed, zooming**) ← regular verb

Adverb

An adverb gives more information about a verb. It limits the word it describes in some way. Adverbs often (but not always) end in "**-ly**". Some examples include: **quickly, happily, suddenly, exactly**.

Preposition

A preposition shows the position of a noun or pronoun. A preposition usually comes before the noun it refers to.

They are often very short words, such as **at, by, in, of, off, on, to** and **up**, but also include such words as **among, before, behind, during** and **through**.

Conjunction

A conjunction is a linking word used to join words, word groups or clauses. They include **and, but, or, yet** and, in pairs and often for emphasis, **both … and, either … or, neither … nor**.

Examples

To help you understand the definitions and parts of speech better we have included phrases that show the words in use (shown in italic in the lines that follow the definitions).

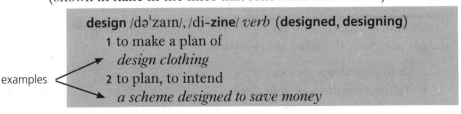

examples <
design /dəˈzaɪn/, /di-**zine**/ *verb* (**designed, designing**)
  1 to make a plan of
   design clothing
  2 to plan, to intend
   a scheme designed to save money

Variations, idioms, phrasal verbs, other common phrases

Words or phrases that are related to the headword are given right at the end of an entry, in bold, with a • at the beginning.

Common phrase

we also give an example to show the phrase in use

> **matter** /ˈmætər/, /**ma-ter**/ *noun*
> • **what's the matter?** asked when there is clearly something wrong
> *you look upset, what's the matter*

Phrasal verb

notice this phrasal verb has two numbered definitions on separate lines

> **dress** /drɛs/, /**dress**/ *verb* (**dressed, dressing**)
> • **dress up**
> 1 to put on the clothing of another person, nation, etc
> *dress up for the fancy-dress party*
> 2 to put on your best clothing
> *dress up for the formal ball*

Idiom

> **elephant** /ˈɛləfənt/, /**e-le-fant**/ *noun*
> • **white elephant** a gift or purchase that turns out to be of no use, a useless possession that is troublesome to keep up or retain

Variations

variations

> **emerge** /iˈmɔrdʒ/, /**i-merge**/ *verb* (**emerged, emerging**)
> • *noun* **emergence** /i-**mer**-jense/
> • *adjective* **emergent** /i-**mer**-jent/

Register

Register is how the word is used in a certain situation or context. The context of how a word is used is shown in the dictionary by labels such as this: *formal, informal, slang, old.*

label showing register

> **bug** /bɐg/, /**bug**/ *noun*
> (*informal*) a hidden microphone used to record other people's conversations secretly

Abbreviations

Words shortened by contracting or that are represented by initials are given the label **abbreviation**.

> **Dr** *abbreviation for* **doctor**
> **TV** *abbreviation for* **television**

The Happy Dog Training Handbook

The Ultimate Guide to Raise a Happy Puppy with Easy Step by Step Methods incl. Bonus: 6 Weeks Training Schedule

Larry K. Stewart

ISBN – 9781697304732

Contents

Introduction

Dog owners around the world have many things in common. One is that they want only the best for their beloved canine. It is easy to feed, play and show your dog how much you love them. However, another important aspect of being a pet owner or parent is dog training.

Efficient training contributes significantly to the health and happiness of dogs. Many people are surprised to learn how important regular activity, discipline and mental health is for dogs. Making the decision to implement training exercises for your dog helps to improve their livelihood dramatically. There are many available options for dog training. The key is to find the proper fit for and your dog to ensure a successful training routine.

Before committing to a dog training routine, know that you have multiple approaches available. There are considerations to be taken to ensure that you are giving your dog the best training available. As a pet parent, you likely know the habits and needs of your dog. This is important to consider when deciding which training approach will be most impactful on your dog.

Depending on the age of your dog, introduction to

training will vary. Puppies can undergo house training as soon as they arrive home, because they are capable of learning at a very young age, from the moment they are born. Training stages vary and include simple to the most complex commands. Obedience training that teaches dogs to sit, stay, fetch and other similar commands can be taught as early as 6 to 8 weeks old.

Formal or professional training is typically held off until after the dog reaches 6 months old. However, it is important to start training during the juvenile phase. It is during this span of life that the puppy is exposed to several experiences, and postponing training for a while may lead to several missed learning opportunities. Young puppies generally begin to pattern the behavior of adults. The best time to address or change any negative patterns is during the puppy stage. Also, any negative habits that a puppy has acquired are easier to reverse when caught early. It is possible and more effective for dogs to learn when they are young.

If training your 6 to 8 week old, use strategies that implement positive support and a gentle approach. Keep the sessions short, as most puppies can only focus for short periods at a time. However, implement some mode of training each day to keep dogs on track with what they're learning to improve their response to it.

For new or long-time dog owners, dog training will become your biggest responsibility regarding your dog. Before beginning the training process, ensure that you have the necessary information and tips to make the process comfortable and effective for your dog. Training that is implemented incorrectly can impose harm or cause setbacks in the obedience development of your beloved dog.

Help Your Dog Adjust to the Idea of Training

The idea of dog training can be overwhelming. Imagine how much of an adjustment it will be for your dog. It's a new process that both parties must adjust to and sometimes, the adjustment is difficult. If you are a novice at this, there will be questions and concerns but following the proper tips and guidelines can alleviate many issues or obstacles before they occur. In addition, take the necessary precautions to make training comfortable for dogs and they will likely respond positively to the training process.

Tips to Help Dogs Adjust to the Training Process

Throw a dog a bone and watch him retrieve it as quick as it left your hand. If only it were this easy to train them about every aspect of obedience. There are multiple ways to encourage a dog to do the right thing, but how do you train them to do it on their own, without being told each time? That's a loaded question for some but for others, it's as simple as helping the dog to adjust to the process and adapt to the fundamentals of training.

Try these suggestions before starting any training approach:

1. **Name that dog**. Most people choose their dog's name based on emotions, childhood memories, or other special considerations. While you can name your dog whatever you choose, a name is iatrical to the entire training process. In training, it is helpful if the dog's name is brief and has a strong ending with a consonant sound. Therefore, when pronounced articulately, the dog hears and understands clearly that he is being addressed. Calling out to Jack – Grover – Buck or Archer will resonate

clearly to dogs and cause them to perk up and pay attention.

2. If your dog is older and already named, you may feel it inappropriate to change it now. Don't pull out the dog name book just yet. This is only if you want to choose something different. Pups from shelters are usually named temporarily and have not become attached to that name. Most breeders give their dogs long names, which may complicate the training process. Rescue dogs that are retrieved from abusive conditions likely have not adjusted to a name or don't respond to anything at all.

3. All these scenarios are capable of being introduced to the possibility of a name change for the dog and it helps to make dogs comfortable with their name and more responsive during training. Whether the name is new or long-term, be sure to associate it to positive and upbeat things, instead of any negative associations. This helps the dog to view his name just as he views other things that make him perk up and feel happy.

4. **Rules of the house**. Prior to brining the dog into the home, determine what rules you'll have in place. Make a list that includes all the rules as they apply to the dog. Will you allow him on the furniture? What areas of the home will he not be allowed in? Where will he be during family dinner time? Establishing what the rules are before the dog comes home makes it easier to enforce them and prevent confusion.

5. **The Dog Cave.** Relax, this is not a suggestion to put your dog in a cave. It's the exact opposite. Just as a man enjoys his man cave, a dog enjoys his own space also. Give him a space that he can feel comfortable in. This will be the area where he sleeps and spend alone time. It's his own little "dog cave" and no one else or other pet should be allowed to occupy that space. Dogs need alone time too. Owners should be rewarded for spending quiet time in their space. In addition, the dog cave (or crate) will be a vital asset in the training process.

6. **Make Him Feel at Home**. Your dog will be the newest member of the household. Make him feel at home when he gets there. Place warm bottle and a clock that ticks in his dog cave. The bottle provides comfort and the clock is like the heartbeat he felt from the litter he left behind. It creates a soothing and relaxing environment that reminds him of what he once knew as a comfortable home. This is especially helpful for

a dog that comes from a loud or busy shelter, or one that was abused.

7. **Answer the Call**. Come Buck! Good dog! Teaching your dog to answer and respond when called is the initial training command to accomplish. Teaching him to answer your call helps to establish your position as the one in charge, the Alpha male. When he responds to the call of his name, get excited and insert some type of constructive reinforcement. Remember, to try this during a time when your dog is occupied with other things or something he's really interested in doing. Once he gets older, you'll begin to notice the advantages of teaching him name commands while he was young.

8. **Good Dog**! It's perfectly acceptable and a great idea to reward your dog when he behaves. Implement toys, cuddles, treats, and other types of praise. Show him that you're pleased with him, and don't reward him for negative behaviour, as it could lead to confusion.

9. **Ignore the jumper**. It's completely common for dogs to jump all over you when they greet you. Never reprimand him. Ignore the jumps and give him time to calm down and then insert constructive reinforcement. Don't pat him or make puppy talk when he jumps on you. Turn the opposite direction and ignore him until he's done jumping up.

10. **Time is Of the Essence**. Of course you know that dogs and puppies are "at the moment" type creatures. They will do a thing, and three minutes later forget it ever happened. Therefore, it's crucial that you reward or discipline them immediately after their act of good deed or defiance. Remaining consistent with acknowledging things as they occur will help dogs to properly associate between the act and the modification.

11. **Bash the biting**. Don't allow him to bite on or nip away at you or items in your home. Don't fuss at him but show him that he's hurting you by mimicking a cry or sadness. This may surprise or shock him and motivate him to stop. If not, give him a toy to chew on. Most refer to this as the "big swap" training method. It can also work when the dog is chewing or biting your clothing, shoes or furniture. Your dog may choose chewing or tossing toys. If neither of these approaches work, stop him from biting and simply ignore him altogether.

12. **Close out sessions positively**. Great job, BOY! End training sessions on a good note. Understand that dogs work hard to get things right, even when you don't think they're taking in the knowledge. They are eager to please their owners. Show them that you are proud of them by praising them, playing with them, or petting them as a reward. This makes him look forward to training sessions because he likes the attention he gets afterwards.

What Really Works in Dog Training

A primary issue with dog training is that owners tend to navigate towards training methods that make them happy. Try to recall that the training process must also generate a good feeling for your dog. Today's dog owners are somewhat stuck on the "positive" approach for training methods. This leads to the use or overuse of food, failure to say "no" to him, or refusal to bestow any feelings of discomfort upon him for his wrong doings.

This is an error that dog owners make when they are stuck on the positive approach. It becomes difficult to ever discipline a dog when you are constantly overlooking their negative behavior. Dogs are smart and will sometimes refuse to obey usually because they are determined and choose not to do so. When this happens, most realize that there are no consequences with owners who never reprimand them for disobeying. Make a habit of verbally saying "No" when your dog disobeys. If he barks nonstop or after you've commanded him to stop, jump on or at people, or do anything that you've warned him against – tell him "NO" assertively.

Remember, raising a dog is similar to raising kids and you don't allow them to get away with bad behavior, do you?

The Downside to the "Just Be Positive" Approach in Dog Training

Yes, the "just be positive" approach when training puppies or dogs is a beneficial thing. But, it's a thing that doesn't work. It's impactful when implementing fun tricks that aren't associated with obedience.

However, when attempting to teach dogs to obey certain commands like sit, stop barking at strangers or to act gently around kids can be challenging if you consistently implement the "just be positive" approach. This approach fails to teach your dog a very important trait, respect. In order to effectively train your dog, he must have respect for you and the commands you give him.

A respectful dog will:

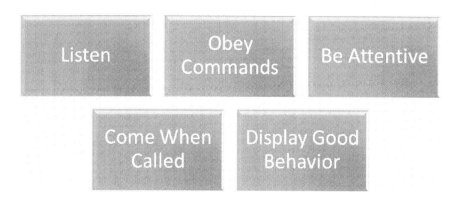

Listen

Obey Commands

Be Attentive

Come When Called

Display Good Behavior

Dogs value respect more than you know. They understand it. It's a stable philosophy of the training process. It is composed of the good and the bad consequences that are associated with the dog's behavior. Everyone, including dogs must be educated and acquire basic learning that teaches them the basics of right and wrong. As humans, if we experience positive moments for a certain behavior, chances are we'll do it again. But, when reprimanded for behaving negatively, it's possible that you will refrain from doing that particular act again. Dogs gain insight from the negative and positive moments they encounter.

It's the "reason and result" factor. When owners are the arbitrator of their dog's conducts – the one who decides what results should occur as a consequence of their reasons – the dog gains respect for their parents.

Once respect is there, they listen and do as they are told, MOST of the time.

Command Words

Expose your dog to gentle, yet consistent discipline. This is often a reflection of their energy and the guidance given by their owners. Also, discipline must also be aligned with a training concept to prevent future behavioral issues.

Here are a few basic commands that when applied properly by owners can be impactful and make being a dog owner easier.

Incorporate these tips before teaching commands:

- Be consistent and exercise understanding and patience
- Teach commands in a calm or quiet environment to prevent being distracted
- Keep sessions brief
- Teach commands on a regular basis until they are learned
- Refrain from incorporating punishments
- Practice training privately before executing demands in public
- Commend the dog for good behavior

- Demonstrate what he should know or do instead of being forceful in your commands

- Move on to a new command once he learns how to execute the old one

- Remember to make learning fun and exciting

- Get involved in the training of commands to show him that you are learning with him

Verbal Word Command List

- **Watch Me –** This command requires you to look your dog in the eyes, show him the treat you have in your hand while moving the treat from his nose to your face. This prompts him to "look from your hand to your face" while you command him to watch you. You can practice this command a few times per day until your canine identifies and recognizes the command. Don't use treats as distractions or to hold his attention. Only offer treats as a reward.

- **Sit –** This command is also taught with a treat to nose movement trick. However, he'll be unable to chase the treat, because he should currently be assuming a natural seated position. This position permits him to raise the head and follow the treat and as he elevates his head, command him to "sit" – along with a treat and a touch of affection. Redo the exercises over and over to make them easier to remember.

- **Down –** Once you've practiced watch me and sit, the "Down" command is easier to work through but can be challenging for dogs to learn. Use a treat in hand and place it near his nose, as soon as he sniffs it, move your hand downward towards the ground or floor for the dog to follow. Now, navigate your hand along the ground to encourage him to go after the food while laying down. Once he's laying down, say the command, "down" and present him with his prize.

- **Stay –** This command is among the most use, even people who don't have dogs will tell stranger's dogs to "stay" when they approach them. Begin the command by telling him (the dog) to sit, place a treat near his nose, and give the command.

- **No –** This command is necessary for both humans and dogs. It is often taught to the latter by inclination of the owners tone and the expression of a firm or discouraging look on the face. If this method isn't effective, pull on the leash and command him to stop by saying "NO" aggressively. Refrain from offering treats when teaching your dog to obey the command.

- **Heel-** Teach this command by having your dog stand near your leg, both of you facing a similar direction. Say the command, heel and move forward a little bit. You want the dog to follow alongside you as you take each step. If he does so correctly, offer him a reward.

- **Leave It** – This is a safety command that every dog should know and understand. To best teach this command, pick up the dog's least favorite treat and encourage him to disregard it. Something like celery will work well, as most dogs don't prefer it. Place it on the floor and make sure he's not attracted to it. Command him to leave it as you place your foot over it. He will likely try to navigate around your foot to get to the item but don't move your footing. After a while, he'll grow tired of trying and won't pay attention to the item anymore. Hence, leaving it alone.

- **Come** – A very basic and commonly used command in the dog world is "come". It can be challenging to get your dog to adjust to this command but it can be done with practice. Allow the dog to run towards a treat you've thrown or just to run out during play with a long leash attached. Gently pull the leash inward while commanding the dog to come. Offer a treat and the dog is surely to come when called. Practice this command using the leash until he becomes accustomed to and obeys the command.

- **Bring/Retrieve It** – This command is easier to teach to pups that are good or know how to retrieve naturally, like the Golden or Labrador breed. However, implementing the same training technique as you do with "come" can be effective when teaching the dog to retrieve or bring an item to you.

- **Catch** – This will be an exciting and entertaining command for owners and their fur babies. It implements play and physical activity into the regimen. Primarily, dogs respond well to the "catch" command. But if not, pass a favorite toy or treat underneath his nose and command him to catch it while mid-air. If he fails to do so, don't give him the treat. The goal is to encourage him to catch the toy or treat while it's in the air.

Hand Signals to Communicate with Your Dog

You should know that for almost every spoken command, there is a verbal command. It is most beneficial to use hand signals in situations where speaking aloud will be inappropriate or perhaps if out hunting.

Hand signals are only effective when the dog is taught to be attentive and friendly towards your verbal instructions. If the plan is to utilize hand signals often, begin with teaching your pup to see and understand what your face is saying and what your body language indicates. Your dog is likely more accustomed to voices and faces. Therefore, you should incorporate a good training technique for hand signals and exercise patience.

Your dog will rely on your facial lingo to coordinate the way they respond or their action with the signals given by your hand. As the dog grows more accustomed to the hand signals, you will be able to eliminate the facial lingo completely.

Many owners are eager to teach dogs tricks and how to respond appropriately to your commands. Once a dog learns the proper training techniques, the training phase is easy and takes just a little block of time each day. One important note is that owners must be comfortable with the verbal or hand commands they're using. In order for your dog to trust you and understand what you want them to do, they must see that you're comfortable giving them the command. You may want to practice the motions for hand signals on your own before engaging the dog with them. Doing so allows you to appear confident and comfortable during training exercises, which leads your dog to trust your facial lingo, voice, and hand motions.

Consistent training is important, but don't stress if you or your dog is not feeling up to it one or two days out of the week. Missing one or two days won't interfere with your training progression. Also, make sure to go over the training commands that were previously learned to keep them in constant mind play and make them easy for the dog to remember when they are given.

Obedience Training

Obedience is significant in life and makes owning a dog much easier. The relationship between pups and people has evolved over time. They are extremely sociable creatures and long for guidance and direction from adults. They want to know how they should act and look to their owners to teach them. Owners have an obligation to educate their dogs by training them and teaching them how and when to socialize.

Why Obedience Training is Necessary

The concept of obedience is to teach your canine simple commands, how to socialize and how they should behave. The available alternatives for teaching canine obedience are expanding. You can enroll him or her in a school to be trained by an experienced trainer, enlist the services of an independent trainer, or implement techniques to train the dog yourself. The advantages are that dogs will sometimes be easier to live with and it eliminates much of the stress associated with ownership. After successful training sessions, you will notice a confident and happier dog.

Here are a few additional benefits of implementing obedience training for your dog.

Manage Him Better

Simple commands that most dogs should be familiar with such as sit, leave it, no, come and watch me are important. They play an important part in helping you to manage your dog better in various situations. These commands are effective in maintaining a safe environment for dogs. Obedience discipline instructs canines to remain calm and display good manners when they encounter others. Positive management enables owners to take their dogs to pet parks, public places, pet-acceptable events and other place. It also keeps you from having to cage your dog or lock him away when visitors are in your home.

Life Saving

A startled dog will easily bolt away from you in fearful situations. Dogs that return to their owners when they are commanded to do so can avoid dangerous situations. If a dog is scared, he may run into oncoming traffic, run away from the space his owner is in or attempt to find shelter to feel safe. A trustworthy command given by his owner will make it easy to manage him when and if he becomes frightened. In the most dangerous situations, an obedient dog will look to his owner to guide him to safety. A well-managed relationship and clarity in training helps dogs to understand who has control and prevents confusion during these situations.

Establishes Understanding

You will enjoy the meaningful time you and your pup have when training him. It requires a great deal of one-on-one time and presents an opportunity for your dog to become familiar with your voice, mannerisms, facial expressions and body language. You are also able to establish the same familiarity with your dog. There is clarity in body language and the development of hand and vocal commands utilized for communication. This provides your dog with the necessary tools to thrive when he is successful at following your commands.

Creates a Bond

It is imperative to create a bond with your dog. Training is a great tool for establishing confidence and respect while creating a bond. If your dog is trained and displays quality manners, he will be easier to manage, comfortable, calm and self-reliant. All these qualities combined present a happy space for you and the dog because you both are clear about the expectations. Research indicates that dogs that have undergone training for obedience are more attentive and in tuned with the commands of owners. This is the foundation for building a strong bond.

Mental Stimulation

By giving your dog the guidance he needs through training, it also provides him with increased physical activity, mental stimulation, quality time and responsibilities. Research indicates that the average dog is more impressed by their reward if they have to work for it or earn it. Your pet feels that it's his responsibility or job to obey those commands and it makes him feel accomplished when he does so successfully.

Teach Your Dog to Not Talk Back to You

You may think it's impossible for dogs to talk back because they're nonverbal. Although they're nonverbal, dogs have a way of talking back or disobeying cOmmands. They can be sassy when they can't have their way.

Dogs are maybe talking back if he displays similar to the following.

- Grumbles or growls when you annoy him (waking him up, moving him off the furniture, taking his favorite item away from him or touching him whenever he'd rather not be touched)

- Stiffens his legs as he tries to hold on to something

- Consistently tugging at the owner while he's busy and not giving him attention

- Takes food off the table or the plate or snoops in the trash when he thinks no one is looking

This is only a brief list of behaviors that dog display when they "talk back" to their masters. It is important to teach them to trust and respect you and to not display disobedient behavior.

Your Dog Must Understand that You Are the Leader

In order to teach a dog obedience and to be respectful, he must first acknowledge that his master is the leader. There are certain characteristics that your dog will display that shows that he accepts and knows who the master is and that's the charge person.

Here are a few signs that your dog acknowledges you as the person in charge of him.

- When someone is at the door, he may bark slightly while stepping back to allow you to approach the door.

- Once the door comes open, he waits for permission to go out instead of bolting outside. This is a show of respect for you.

- He is easy to manage on when walking on a slack leash and looks at you occasionally to determine which direction he should be going.

- Once a strange person or other dog approaches your space, he may look towards you to give the okay to advance without fear.

You are in charge of your dog learning to obey and seeing to it that he follows through with the lessons in obedience that you've provided him. The bond established between owner and pup is one that instils trust, respect and motivates the pup to be guided by you. This is the type of relationship that allows dogs to flourish and lead happy lives.

Dogs Need to Feel Secure.

1. **It instils a comfort within**. Dogs feel safe when they know that they have someone to follow. Dogs want to have someone in a leadership position to provide them guidance. It's a big relief that they can trust their master to make all the major decisions in life.

2. **It allows them to feel loved**. Dogs that are willing to follow you are also willing to listen to your commands. This makes it easier to instil positive behaviour in them. When they behave appropriately, it motivates praise from others, which excites most dogs. They recognize when their masters are pleased with them by their voice pitch and facial expressions.

3. **It allows them to accompany their owners in public more often**. If a dog displays good behavior away from home, their master will take them out with them more often. Obedience is important because it prevents the dog from being left behind or caged when guests are around.

4. **They recognize that there are consequences for their action.** Dogs are aware that when they behave properly, they receive praise and rewards. They are also aware that bad behavior results in negative consequences. This awareness leads an obedient dog to make good behavior choices more often than not.

5. **They are familiar with the human tone and what it means.** Obedience training teaches dogs to recognize the human voice and its various pitches. They can tell the difference between a confident owner and one that is doubtful about their ability to lead. They can also tell the difference between a voice of praise and one of discipline.

Socializing Your Dog

You want your dog to be sociable because it makes it easier for him to be around others without feeling anxious or fretful. All dogs aren't social butterflies and some will have to endure obedience training before learning the significance of interacting with others. Dogs should be comfortable when in the presence of other dogs and humans.

Human Socialization

Dogs become more comfortable around humans when they are exposed to environments where there is a high presence of humans. These are great tips to help introduce human socialization to your dog.

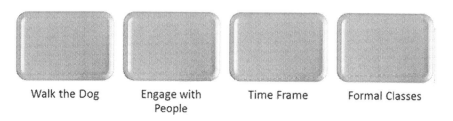

Walk the Dog   Engage with People   Time Frame   Formal Classes

Walk the Dog – Visit a public park to walk him around, which exposes him to human interaction. It helps him to become familiar with sounds and people such as car horns, heavy traffic, the mailman and more. Be sure to use a little leash, and take various routes when walking, which exposes him to different people.

Engage with People – Dogs should be exposed to a wide variety of people. Be sure to take them around men, women, and children. This allows him to become accustomed to the concept of interacting with all types of people. Dogs that are only exposed to a few of the same people may be guarded around anyone but those people. Therefore, it's important to schedule several outings with your dog that include a quality mix of people.

Incorporate these human interaction/introduction tips:

- Remain calm and poised when the dog appears skittish around others. Don't force or make a fuss about his stand-offish behavior.

- When petting, tell others to keep their hands visible to the dog. Suggest the chin or chest area.

- Incorporate treats into the meet and greet with strangers and the dog.

- Consider the services of a dog walker to expose the dog to other people during the walk.

Socialization Time Table

Puppies adjust better when socialized between the ages of 3 to 11 weeks.

Expose your 3-11 week old puppies to some of the following:

- Strangers
- Unfamiliar clothing such as hats, hoodies, or sunglasses
- Strange environments
- Wooded areas or bodies of water
- Automobiles
- Variety of floor surfaces and outdoor ground
- Community signs
- Bicycles
- Motorcycles or scooters
- Cats
- Other trained dogs

Once a dog is four months or older, socialization may be more challenging, but still possible. You should attempt the task even with older canines. In most instances, you need to motivate your pup to adapt to the process and proceed at a pace that is comfortable for him.

Signs of anxiety in your dog may include:

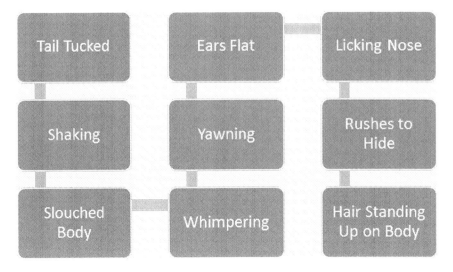

Forcing a young puppy into situations that are uncomfortable before they are prepared may lead them to feel anxious and become withdrawn. It can also lead them to form negative connotations with the very thing you're attempting to make them accustomed to. You should progress slowly and lead your canine from somewhat challenging to aggressively challenging experiences.

The Impact of Negative Experiences

Negative encounters could make your dog feel inclined to behave aggressively as a defense mechanism when they feel threatened.

Familiarize yourself with the body language that your canine displays. Such as:

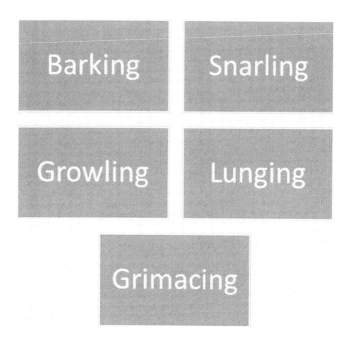

Barking Snarling

Growling Lunging

Grimacing

When your dog presents signs such as the ones above, you likely need to combine socialization training with other fundamentals of training. You may need to consult with a professional dog handler or trainer, or participate in a group training session.

Pay close attention to your dog's reaction when he's around unfamiliar people. It is possible for him to be cautious but not necessarily defensive. If this happens, slowly introduce them in an encouraging manner.

Socializing a Rescue Canine

It's possible to socialize your rescue canine also. Keep this tips in mind.

1. **Keep interactions positive**. Give the dog praise and consistent encouragement. Avoid using treats when having your dog engage or interact with other dogs. This prevents the possibility of a squabble over the treat. Reward him for facing or interacting with the thing that scares him. Don't force interaction.

2. **Keep interactions brief.** When engaging in on-leash encounters, once you notice that the other canine if friendly, let yours sniff, give him praise and only allow them to interact for a half-minute or less. Once you have left the dog, offer your dog a treat as a reward for the positive interaction. Staying around the other dog for too long could lead your dog to feel uncomfortable.

3. **Keep encounters simple.** Refrain from adding more stress to your canine. A relaxed dog absorbs information and learns eagerly and easily. When exposed to stressful circumstance, teaching them may present multiple challenges. If the objective is to have your dog feel comfortable when walking down a crowded street, begin by walking him on a quiet neighborhood street. Once they are comfortable with that, move on to a somewhat busier street.

Observe Your Dog to Better Understand His Feelings

It's important to know how your dog is feeling in certain environments or situations. This is a big part of teaching him to be sociable. Try to observe and understand his body language. This helps you to control almost any situation, expected or surprising.

Indirect body language and expressions on the face show the thoughts and feelings of dogs. You should be attentive to these things from the very start. Observe them closely to become more conversant with them. You will learn important details that will enable you to properly handle him in all situations. The more you learn, the easier it will become for you to identify ad respond to his expressions. The more you know, the more available you are to contribute to his mental, expressive and psychological well-being.

Positive Reinforcement

Dog training works to implement positive reinforcement when done correctly. It's commonly referenced as non-forced, reward stipulated, or click/treat (C/T) training. Under either name, positive reinforcement works to let your dog know when he's done something correctly, and not just point out the mistakes or his misbehaviors.

Quality positive reinforcement uses markers for accuracy and timing, along with rewards, which act as reinforcement for your dog. Markers can be any device that makes a particular sound when activated, or simply use brief words like "yes," or "good."

The Reward Process

Rewards are considered prizes whether they are food or other valued items. A treat such as high-quality chewables or dog food is considered high value, while kibble would be considered or viewed as low value. You can also incorporate rewards such as toys, gentle petting, praise, or fun play, or whatever your dog is enthusiastic about working for.

Once the proper behavior is displayed, mark it at once. The reward is given after the marker. This teaches the dog to link the marker to the reward in his mind, resulting in positive endings in the dog's behavior.

The Concept of Positive Reinforcement

Operant acclimatizing is the process that supports the psychological concept of positive reinforcement. It is a method of learning that incorporates the addition or removal of a punishment or prize. This leads to the surge or decline of a particular behavior. Positive reinforcement focuses on the presentation of a reward or prize to improve the chances of a certain behavior.

The concept generated in 1940 by psychologist, B.F. Sinner. However, it wasn't introduced in training until the 90s. Since its comeback, it has taken its place as a staple in the training process for animals and growing in popularity.

Many believe that PR overpowers the concept of traditional training strategies, which are centered control and punishment. Instead of scaring a dog into learning, positive reinforcement training encourages him to act appropriately because it's exciting and extremely rewarding.

This is also a bond-builder for the dog and its owner. It establishes clear lines of respect and unwavering trust, which allows clarity in communication. Trainers also notice an improvement in the dog's eagerness to work, please, and improved frequency of learning.

The Art of Calming Signals

Dog owner or not, a calm dog is a pleasure for anyone to encounter. It reduces the stress of the interaction and presents an opening for the dog to engage with others. It is even more important for dogs to remain calm when around each other. They need this experience in order to hunt, raise their pups, and to interact appropriately with each other. When dogs engage in an environment that is not calm, it can lead to physical injuries or disappointment to the master.

Dogs are extremely perceptive of the little things. A sudden change of behavior, a rapid signal or an unpleasant facial expression are all noticed quickly by dogs. There are approximately 25-30 signals that dogs display to their owners or others around them. You should be familiar with what they are in order to properly train and socialize your dog. It's easy to mistake these signals for inappropriate behavior. Doing so could create a barrier between or break the established connection that you have with your pup.

Understand That Signal

Yawning (calming for the dog)

Dogs often yawn if:

- a person bends down near or over them
- when their master signs agitated
- if there's yelling or an argument
- at the veterinarian
- when someone is approaching them
- when they are excited or eager about something
- when told to do something they don't want to do
- during long training exercises
- when told NO

Licking (calming)

- Licking is a calming effort that is often displayed by dogs that are covered in hair, especially on the face
- Most black dogs lick to calm themselves
- Tongue tip quickly brushes against the nose
- Licking signal is often used as communication between dogs

Head Turn

- Dog tilts head slightly to the left or right (someone approaches from front, if someone is angry)

- Turns head fully over to the left or right (someone bends over to stroke him)

- Turns body fully and the tail faces the person being calmed (extensive training lessons, when someone surprises him0

Bow Down and Play

Another signal that dogs use is bending forward on their front legs and maneuvering legs from one side to the other. This can be used to signal another dog to come and play. Other times, when the dog stands firm as he bows down it can be in an attempt to calm a person down. There are alternate or multiple meanings for some signals.

Sniffing

You will often observe a dog sniffing or smelling the ground, especially a pack of pups. Dogs often sniff or put their nose to the ground when:

- Someone approaches their handler

- Busy environments

- Noisy environments

- When they notice something unfamiliar on the ground

Walking at a Slow Pace

Brisk walking may seem too aggressive to your dog and they may be tempted to stop whoever is walking rapidly or running. This is a hunting instinct that may be triggered as soon as a dog or human approaches them running or walking at a fast pace. It's a natural mechanism of defense for dogs.

Timid dogs will move or walk at a slow pace. If you want to help your dog to feel confident and safe, move or walk at a slow pace. Once a dog initiates a calming effort, moving slowly will help to relax them.

A Calm Dog Can Sleep All Night

Are you wondering if you will get enough or any sleep at all with your dog roaming the house or growling all night? You don't have to wonder any longer. You could train your dog to sleep while you do throughout the night. In the beginning, don't expect to you or your dog to sleep a full night. However, incorporating a few positive training tips could afford you a full night's sleep sooner than later.

Consider these tips to help you and your dog sleep peacefully through the night.

Starter Crate – you may have looked forward to your dog sleeping with you but at first, he won't be doing much sleeping during the night. To help you get more rest than you would with him roaming around or pulling your covers, put him in a crate to start out. Once he's adopted healthy sleep habits, you can move him to the bed if you wish.

Before you allow your canine to nap or sleep in your bed overnight make sure that he is:

- Completely potty trained

- Sleeps peacefully at night

- Adjusted to the crate and understands what it's used for

Create a Comfortable Space – your dog may seem apprehensive about falling asleep at night, but when they decide to go they want to be comfortable. Create a comfortable crate or space by adding fluffy blankets or similar items. Make sure that all materials used for the dog's sleeping space are comfortable and pet-friendly. Align the bottom of the crate with fluffy, soft and oversize towels. There are dog beds and soft pads available for your dog.

Physical Activity – Engage your dog in lots of physical activity and exercise, especially late evening just before he goes down for bed. Playing with your dog helps to tire him out and motivates him to sleep well at night. Remember to:

- Let him outside for about 30 minutes to walk before bed

- Exercise his mind during the night by working on training skills

- Spend about 30 minutes in high energy play before bed

Bedtime Snack – though he shouldn't eat a heavy meal just before bedtime, you should allow him to have a small snack or meal two or three hours before he goes down for bed. This prevents him from waking up after a few hours due to hunger.

Bathroom Run – take your dog for one last bathroom run prior to going to bed. This presents a greater chance that he'll sleep through the night without needing to go to the bathroom. This will also decrease the chances of you having a messy bed pad or crate to clean the following day.

Nighttime Routine - just like humans, your dog needs a routine that he can stick to at night. Developing a routine helps your dog to understand that bedtime is approaching. The night treat, playtime and nighttime potty trip are great routines to lead up to bedtime. Consistency is key when developing a routine that the dog will enjoy.

Cuddle Companion - your dog will sleep more comfortably if you give him something to cuddle. A cuddly blanket or stuffed dog pillow are perfect for cuddling and comfort. Once the dog becomes accustomed to it, he may want to have it in any area that he sleeps. The blanket or pillow could also work as an attraction to the area that is designated as the dog's sleep space. He'll know that this is the area he's supposed to sleep.

Relaxing sounds and scenery - create a space that motivates your dog to sleep through the night. Find puppy scents that your dog love and add them to the sleep space or crate. Play his favorite tunes or sounds to help him relax and fall asleep. Essential scents like lavender are relaxing and playing white noise is a suggestion for the dog who needs help sleeping throughout the night.

Turn Down the Lights – Melatonin is beneficial and extremely popular for contributing to healthy sleep patterns of humans and dogs. It's a hormone that induces sleep and if the lights are off or turned down, melatonin production rises. So, turn the lights down in the area where your dog sleeps.

Dog Training Basics

Basic Care and Training Goals

Check the box as the goal is achieved:

Dietary

Good Quality Diet and Food – no corn, by products, wheat, artificial colors or preservatives	
Supplement with healthy additives such as fresh vegetables, meat and yogurt	
Avoid or limit intake of junk food	

Handling/Grooming Checklist

Practice touching or patting daily to make dog comfortable (on the feet, tail and ears)	
Dog appears relaxed when being brushed	

Brush regularly to maintain healthy skin and to prevent the coat from matting	
Dog is relaxed while ears are being cleaned	
Clean the ears weekly	
Dog is okay with receiving baths	
Dog should be bathed once each month	
Dog is okay with getting his teeth brush	
Dog's teeth should be brushed once each month	

Exercise and Outside Activities

Dog has several toys to keep him entertained and active	
Dog has one (at least) favorite toy	
Dog is exercised by someone for at least half an hour each day	
Dog undergoes 10 minutes of training daily	

Avoid possessiveness by making sure:

Dog accepts someone touching his sleep pad, feeding bowl or toys	
Dog doesn't mind other humans or dog having access to his master	

Comfortable Vehicle Ride

Dog should be relaxed while riding in vehicle	
Dog should be restrained properly in vehicle	

Miscellaneous

Get at least 10 hours of quality sleep	
Maintain regular veterinarian visits and maintain scheduled vaccinations	
Your dog should be treated; spayed/neutered	
Maintain a healthy weight	
Dog should not remain outside for too many hours without supervision	
Dog should be having few to no accidents inside each week	
Avoid extreme treatments of parasite	

Dog Training with a Clicker

You have multiple unique training tools available to simplify the training process. Clickers are among the many tools that owners or masters can incorporate into the dog training process. It is a tiny device used in the training process. Just as the name suggests, it makes a unique sound when clicked. It is clicked to inform the dog that he has done a good thing and will receive a treat. This can be for any good act performed by the dog such as letting something go upon command or sitting when told to do so.

Clickers are used in training sessions to encourage the dog to achieve tasks or succeed and prevent behaviors that aren't good. Training objectives are typically categorized into little, achievable methods. Clickers do not incorporate punishment into the teaching process.

It is always easy to just say "good dog" or "yes" but the clicker works quicker. Once the dog comprehends what he has been taught, the clicker can be put away and verbal recognition can be given.

How Do Treats Impact Diet

Many dog owners fear that rewarding their dogs with treats may impede their diet or make them fat. You shouldn't give meal-size treats. Therefore, you're not worried about over treating them or making them fat. A treat should be given in a size equivalent to that of a pea and always subtract it from the dog's daily portion allowance. You can even incorporate his meal food into inside training as a reward instead of a snack treat. Use healthy foods for rewards.

You don't have to use treats for rewards all the time. They are a great option during the initial introduction of the clicker. Remember to be certain the dog responds or follows-through properly with your instructions before treating him to a reward. A reward can be almost anything your dog values or gets excited about. Never show the treat first. With the clicker approach, the reward follows the execution of proper behavior.

Inside the Treat Bag

What type treats are you giving your dog? It matters! Keep the following tips in mind.

- Treats should be easily to access when needed (fits in a pocket or pouch) and about the size of a pea

- When training in a loud environment, give the good treats. Cheerios work great for indoors but the amount of work the dog does on the outside calls for the good stuff like dried liver or cubed cheese.

- Mix the treats up to keep the concept of surprise for the dog

- Treat suggestions:
    o Diced luncheon meat (you can dry the meat by placing it in the microwave 3 times for 20-30 seconds between two paper towels)
    o Cheese (shredded)
    o Cream cheese or peanut butter is a nice grooming treat (allow the dog one lick per good behavior
    o Cheerios or similar cereal
    o Dry dog food
    o Dry liver
    o Dry jerky
    o Carrots

- o Popcorn
- o Apple slices
- o Meat-like baby food
- o Commercial treats for dog (avoid artificial flavors or preservatives)
- o Ice chips

The Command Guide

Dog Responds to His Name

1. Arrange a nice assortment of treats and place them in a pouch or your pocket

2. Call your dog by his name. Once he lays eyes on you, hit the clicker and give him a treat

3. Practice this all around the house, with him leashed, outdoors, during a walk, in the park, when visitors are over, when their favorite foods and treats are visible, when in a crowded place, etc. Your dog's response to his name being called is perhaps the most important aspect of training you will instil in him. It's the basis of every other training concept. In addition, it prepares your dog to avoid trouble.

4. Reward voluntary eye contact from the dog by using the click and treat method.

5. Use the following chart to manage your advancement.

Check the item off once your dog has made eye contact with you 8/10 of the times you call him by name (without luring him):

Make eye contact with me when we are:

Inside the home without distractions	
Outdoors in backyard without distractions	
Inside the home with low impact distractions	
Outside in the backyard with low impact distractions	
Inside the home with mediocre distractions	
Outside in the backyard with mediocre distractions	
Inside the home with an extreme degree of distractions	
Outside in the backyard with an extreme degree of distractions	

Types of distractions:

Low impact: Another person present in the training area

- You have an item inside your hand while training

Mediocre level: Doorbell or phone sounds off while training

- Making the command while in an unfamiliar position (bending over)

- Making the command while in an area different than other times

- You have a treat displayed visibly inside your hand

Extreme degree: Humans, dogs or other pets engaging while giving the command

- Tossing a ball

- In a busy area such as a park

- While friends are over

Dog Responds to Come

"COME" is a highly utilized safety tools with dogs. It's important to train your dog to run your way whenever you command him to come. This command will deem helpful in the event your dog leaves home unattended. Upon finding him, commanding him to "come" will prompt his return

Check the item off once your dog Comes to you upon your command 8/10 of the times that you command him to (without luring him):

Inside the home without distractions	
Outside in the backyard without distractions	
Inside the home with low impact distractions	
Outside in the backyard with low impact distractions	
Inside the home with mediocre distractions	
Outside the home with mediocre distractions	
Inside the home with extreme level distractions	
Outside the home with extreme level distractions	

Types of distractions:

Low impact: Another person present in the training area

- You have an item inside your hand while training

Mediocre level: Doorbell or phone sounds off while training

- Making the command while in an unfamiliar position (bending over)

- Making the command while in an area different than other times
- You have a treat displayed visibly inside your hand

Extreme degree: Humans, dogs or other pets engaging while giving the command

- Tossing a ball
- In a busy area such as a park
- While friends are over

Dog Responds to Leave It

Check the item off once your dog Leaves It upon your command 8/10 of the times that you command him to do so (without luring him):

Less valued item inside your hand	
Highly valued item inside your hand	
Two items on floor (less favored and highly favored)	
Two items on floor (less favored and highly favored) while you stand away from them	
Walk past object, leashed indoors and outdoors	
Item tossed or dropped indoors or outdoors	
Live object indoors or outdoors	
Object for one or more minutes	

Example items:

Least favored: Cheerios

Most favored: Rawhide

Check the item off once your dog "Sits" upon your command 8/10 of the times that you command him to (without luring him):

Inside the home without distractions
Outside in the backyard without distractions
Inside the home with low impact distractions
Outside in the backyard with low impact distractions
Inside the home with mediocre distractions
Outside the home with mediocre distractions
Inside the home with extreme level distractions
Outside the home with extreme level distractions

Types of distractions:

Low impact: Another person present in the training area

- You have an item inside your hand while training

Mediocre level: Doorbell or phone sounds off while training

- Making the command while in an unfamiliar position (bending over)

- Making the command while in an area different than other times

- You have a treat displayed visibly inside your hand

Extreme degree: Humans, dogs or other pets engaging while giving the command

- Tossing a ball

- In a busy area such as a park

- While friends are over

Help Your Dog Become Comfortable With Being Handled

This section will instruct your dog to stay immobile and wait for his reward during handling. Handling can be executed for medical purposes or during grooming. It is also designed to teach him to receive accidental incorrect handling. This behavior is highly important and necessary for your dog to comprehend. It helps him to remain calm and avoid aggression.

Reminders:

- Never use the clicker next to your dog's head.

- Once he has comprehended the proper handling techniques, allow him to engage the strategies with others.

- Placing peanut butter or a similar treat down on your floor is a type of motivation that helps the dog to remain still during handling, even if he hasn't had any training on being still yet.

- If the dog is not a fan of handling, the upcoming method when executed slowly can teach him to adjust to it easier. Allow another person, perhaps a professional to groom him until he is comfortable with that handling process. You may want to introduce the use of a muzzle until he becomes comfortable with the process.

- Incorporate handling training for up to two minutes a few times per week to help him become comfortable with the process.

For each exercise, insert the following:

Start with brief, respectful touches. If the dog remains still and doesn't try to move away, click and follow with a treat. If he tries to move away, continue to rub him, however don't force him to stay. Use sticky hands, which means your hands will remain on the dog even if he moves away until he stays still. Once still, you should click and follow up with a treat, then let him go.

- Don't move to another step before the dog is comfortable with the existing step.

- Only try these strategies for a few minutes

Helping the dog to warm-up to handling on various areas of the body:

1. **Collar**: Retreat to a quiet practice area with the clicker, goody treats and the dog.

   a. Touch the collar underneath the chin area and let him go immediately while clicking and treating. Repeat this step approximately 8 or 9 times until he is okay with your doing this.

   b. Grab his collar underneath the chin area for about 3 seconds. Continue to do this until your dog is okay with you doing so and then slowly increase the time 8 to 10 seconds.

   c. Put your hand on the collar underneath his chin area and pull on it a little. C/T if he doesn't resist. If he attempts to move away, gently hold his collar until the dog calms down and then let the collar go. Then, click and treat. Keep doing so until your dog responds as you wish. Move on to attempt similarly, but this time place your hand above the collar. Modify intensity levels and duration throughout practice.

2. **Ears**:

   a. Reach along the right or left areas of the head and rub the dog's ear. Click and treat if he accepts it. Repeat this at least 8 or 9 times.

   b. Once he accepts the touching of his ear, try holding it for at least a second. If he tries to escape the touch, continue to hold the ear, but walk with him as he tries to move away from you. Once he stays in place, click, treat and release. Continue this routine until he allows you to grasp the ear for at least 10 seconds.

c. Practice handling his ear and act like you're cleaning that area. Rub slowly to allow the dog to enjoy the process. After a few days of doing this routines, he should accept it and not attempt to move away. If he has sensitive ears, it could take a little while longer for him to adjust.

3. **Dog Paws**:

Dogs can be extremely delicate around the paw area. You should approach this handling session slowly to allow him to enjoy it and be more accepting of this. Never attempt to trim his nails unless you are experienced at this. One short clip and it may be painful for your dog. With all of these handling strategies, if he's accepting, click and treat, but if he attempts to move away from you, stay with him and only click and treat once he stops trying to move away from you. It should take a few days to complete each step in this handling strategy with numerous repetitions. Be sure to master one step completely before moving forward to the next one. Each exercise should be practiced with each paw (4).

a. Lift up the dog's paw and click and treat immediately. Do this 5 or 6 times before moving on to cuddle (hold) the paw for just a second.

b. Hold each paw for 8 to 10 seconds without resistance from him.

c. Grasp the paw. Then rotate it around making a circular motion.

d. Caress his paw.

e. Act as if you're trimming the dog's nails.

4. **Tail**: Keep in mind that most dogs are extremely sensitive about their tails

   a. Touch his tail briefly. Do so 8 to 10 times incorporating the click/treat method. When he appears comfortable with this, move on and hold it for approximately 10 seconds.

   b. Complete these steps slowly: Lift the tail in an upward direction while brushing and tugging it gently.

5. **Mouth**:

   a. Lightly touch his mouth and then, click and treat. Repeat this step 10 times.

   b. Touch his mouth on the side; gently pull on one lip to reveal a single tooth. Click and treat and let go only after the dog isn't resisting the handling exercise.

c. Progress slowly and: lift his lip to show even more teeth, on each side and move on to open his mouth.

6. **Lifting**: It is sometimes necessary for you to lift a dog, especially during an emergency. Begin by placing the arms around him for brief periods using clicks/treats and next, move on to lift the dog from the ground. You can also practice this during grooming appointments as you lift him onto the table.

7. A Child's Touch:

a. Greet the dog with touches similar to those a kid may engage. Be sure to supervise kids as they interact with any dog to keep them both safe. Practice this strategy by clicking and treating the dog for being accepting of the unfamiliar touches of kids. These touches may include tugs at the ear or tail, or quick pats on the head and sometimes a hug. Progress slowly with this handling training exercise.

Leash Etiquette

Picture yourself walking your dog along next to you and he always stops whenever you do, turns whenever you do and walks past other humans and dogs without delay. There's no pulling away from you and the dog only uses the bathroom or sniffs the ground with permission. These are among the most difficult behaviors to teach your fur baby but it can be fun to do. Continue reading to learn how to simplify the approach to teach your dog leash etiquette.

Head collars or a harness that attaches at the front are great tools that work to deter the dog and keep him from pulling. However, he will need to undergo training to teach him to walk alongside you and not pull while doing so.

Harnesses that attach at the front are simple to use and safe. It's an ideal tool to use with almost any type of dog. If your dog displays aggressive behavior or need extra control during handling training, you should consider the use of a head collar. This is a great collar for owners who are petite but own large dogs. You must pair a leash that is no longer than 6 feet in length with this collar and harness. A leash that is longer than 6 feet could cause the dog to become injured if he met one end of the short leash suddenly.

An easy approach to teaching a dog to walk while not tugging at the leash would be to quit walking forward as he pulls away. Then, once the dog makes his way to your side and walks as he should, treat him.

These detailed steps will assist you in instructing your dog on proper leash etiquette.

STEP 1: SOMETHING SMELLS YUMMY!

Attach a non-retractable leash (10-20 ft. long) with the dog embraced in a standard type harness. Use tiny pieces of meat or cubes of cheese as rewards and take him to an outside area that he's familiar with.

Choose to let him walk alongside you on the right or left and give him a treat next to your thigh on the side that you're walking him on. Eventually, he will take to that particular side because that's where the delicious treats are hidden.

Walk vigorously and casually around the yard. Once the dog decides to walk alongside you, click and treat him alongside the thigh that you've guided him to walk next to. If the dog continues to walk alongside you, continue to click/treat with each step taken. As he progresses in this process, it won't be necessary to treat him as often as it is in the beginning.

Practice this routine until your dog begins to naturally walk alongside you almost every time you walk with him.

STEP 2: I LOVE TO GO WHERE MY MASTER GOES.

Start out in your backyard. Wait until the dog strays to another area of the yard or begins to sniff the ground. Firmly say to him "let's go" while slapping your hand against your thing a couple times to ensure he notices that you have given the command. Then, go in the direction that is opposite of where the dog is at that moment.

If your dog reaches you prior to the leash tightening, click/treat by giving him a couple treats to your favored side and click and treat for each two steps taken, as long as he walks alongside you.

If the canine doesn't respond to your "let's go" command and the leash is tight, stop moving but add a bit of leash pressure. Once he navigates towards you, acknowledge how good he's done and allow a little slack in the leash. Once he reaches you, don't click/treat him but instead, command him to "let's go" once more while he's paying attention to you. Click and treat once he moves alongside you with every two to three steps.

Repeat this step as long as he remains at your side the majority of the time during the walk in the yard and if he walks away from you, remember to say "let's go" to persuade your pup to return to you.

STEP 3: TO SNIFF OR POTTY, THAT'S THE QUESTION.

When walking dogs on a leash, they will sometimes need to use the bathroom and sniff. Help your dog determine the right time to do both. When practicing walking on a leash, approximately every 6 or 7 minutes, or when you would typically click/treat, instruct him to sniff and allow him to walk around with nose to the ground. You can do the same while telling him to go potty, while leashed. Both these are privileges, and if the dog tugs at the leash during free time tell him to "let's go" while walking away, which indicates that free or playtime has ended.

STEP 4: I SHOULD BE MORE ATTENTIVE TO MY MASTER TO SEE WHERE HE'S GOING.

Continue with walking the dog on a leash around the yard, just as in the steps above but this time with a short leash. You will eventually reduce the lease to 6 feet.

Practice taking rapid or slow steps, instantly stopping or going in different directions. Click and treat your dog if he can remain alongside you with each challenge.

You will click and treat him less often the more familiar he becomes with the process. You should click and treat him when a task is difficult for him, especially if it was a challenging task due to direction change or some form of distractions.

Street Smarts:

During walks around the neighborhood, apply the strategies you employed in your backyard, but expect there to be more challenges and distractions. These distractions include friendly but unknown people, squirrels, traffic and dogs. The use of a harness with a front-attachment along with a head collar will give you more control during the walk. Don't forget to bring quality treats such as meat and cubed cheese.

Say "let's go" and move in the opposite direction when the dog isn't noticing you, give him a treat as he walks next to you. Extra treats are a nice when the environment is noisy or difficult to pay attention in. Remember to allow him to take a break and sniff.

Stop and Go Exercise:

Pair an average harness with a leash (6 ft.). Holding the leashed dog, throw the dog's ball or a favorite treat approximately 15 or 20 ft. away from you both.

If he navigates toward the item, tell him "let's go" as you turn to walk in the other direction. If the dog walks alongside you as you move towards it, let him move towards it until he makes it to the object and can retrieve it as a treat.

To simplify the training strategy for the dog, attach a leash that has more length or use a less favorable item.

Helpful Tips:

If the dog attempts to crossover your position, stomp your feet to alert him of your presence.

If he lingers behind, he could be experiencing fear or not up to the task. Be encouraging and don't try to pull the dog alongside you. If the dog delays to sniff or use the potty, you should continue walking as you apply a little pressure to the leash.

Remember to treat your walk when he walks when and where he's supposed to.

The following chart can help with the assessment of your dog's leash etiquette progress:

Check the box when each item is successfully achieved approximately 85% of the time (without luring):

Walks calmly (without lagging) alongside you as you...	
Walk your grounds with a leash (approx.. 10ft)	
Walk around the yard with a leash (approx....6ft)	
Take a walk in the community during its quietest hours for approximately 5 minutes	
Take a walk in the community during busier hours for approximately 10 minutes	
Take a walk in the community during busy hours for approximately 20 minutes	
Walk in the park	
Walk around the pet store	

Housetraining Basics

If you remember nothing else about housetraining your dog, remember this important note – no mistakes allowed.

When housetraining, we focus on the concept that dogs have strong considerations in regards to where they go potty and can develop some solid habits. It is imperative to avoid accidents. Each time your dog goes potty inside the house, he is becoming attached to doing so in this space. Whenever this happens, it's YOUR fault but don't be too hard on yourself. Until a dog is clear on where to and where not to potty, he must be watched constantly, inside his crate, or on a comfortable pad. The dog crate should have just enough space for the dog to lay down and turn around comfortably. If frequent accidents are occurring in the crate, it may be larger than it should be. When inside the home and the dog is not in his crate, tether the pup to your waist area and keep a close eye on him to observe behavior such as circling or sniffing. If you see this, take the dog outside at once. Set an alarm to sound off every hour to remind you to take the dog out on a schedule. As progression is made, this time can be moved up in 30 minute increments. If the dog doesn't go potty when taken out and a few hours have passed, return inside and bring him back out again after 15 minutes.

Set a schedule and stick to it.

A dog should be taken out several times throughout the day. Most often after he's eaten, had playtime or a nap. Feed him between 2 and 3 times each day. Allow food to remain on the floor for approximately 15-20 minutes each feeding. You can leave the water bowl out until 8:00 pm. Dogs can typically hold their ability to go for as long as their age (months) and 1 hour, up to a maximum of 8 hours for adults. Brining your dog out from the start works better, as it helps to minimize the opportunities for accidents and gives the dog more chances to be rewarded for doing as he should.

Consistently simple is key.

Until the dog is really trained, take him to the same potty spot each trip, and always leave some waste behind. This is the designated potty area, and shouldn't be used to play in. Using the leash, take your pup out and say with a firm voice, "hurry up" once you notice him preparing to potty. As he relieves himself, don't distract him, but once he's done click or give him some praise. You can also give him a nice treat and allow him to play (not in or near the potty space) outside for about 5 minutes. If he doesn't potty, go back inside the house, place him in the crate and try again 15 minutes later.

What happens if your dog goes potty inside the house?

Tap yourself across the head with a wad of newspaper because it's your fault! Once you notice that a dog is going potty in the wrong area, rush him outside and pat him or give him a treat for finishing in his outdoor space. If there is a mess, clean it up but don't let him see you. Utilize pet-safe cleaners to remove the stains.

How to train my dog to let me know when he has to go potty?

Place a bell close to the door the dog goes out to potty. Smear peanut butter on a small area of the bell and whenever it rings after the dog touches it, open the door immediately. Do this each time you let him out to potty and before long, he will ring the bell with no peanut butter in sight. This teaches your dog to let you know whenever he has the urge to get outside. Remember to take her out to potty whenever he rings the bell. If he doesn't need to potty after a few minutes have passed, take him back inside. The bell should be used as a signal to use the bathroom only.

Housetraining Tracker

Date & Time	PeePee	Poopie	On demand?	Feeding	Misc.

Date & Time	PeePee	Poopie	On demand?	Feeding	Misc.

The Barker

Dogs will bark for a variety of reasons. Many of the common reasons follow with a few suggestions for solving the issue that leads to the barking.

Needs attention:

Your dog may bark if he wants you to feed or play with him. Whatever he wants, don't give in when he barks to get your attention. Doing so could lead him to think that you'll give in to his wants whenever he barks. Say the command "leave it" without looking at or acknowledging his presence. You could even walk into another space or room, closing the door behind you. Once he stops barking and calms down, you can then do what it is he wishes you would do. Try to initiate games and activities that your dog prefers and add them to your daily schedule. Be sure that everything your dog gets is earned and not just given. Ensure that he "sits" to receive a reward or privilege like outdoor play, getting leashed or his food dish, etc.

He sees something or hears and interesting sound:

When at home:

1. Stop: Cover the source of the sound or what he sees. Use a fan, blinds or move him to another space in the home.

2. Instruct him to be QUIET:

- When he barks, wave a treat or food across his nose and say, QUIET. Once he ends the bark to smell his treat, click/treat. Once you've tried this about three times, next barking episode, act like you have a treat in hand and say QUIET. Once he quietens, C/T. Click and treat at 6 or 7 second intervals and keep doing so while he stays quiet after the cue is given. Slowly raise the elapsed time between each click.

- Reward your dog for being quiet without being told to do so when he's around something that typically causes him to bark.

- Give a time out.
  - o Don't give time outs too often. Taking your dog away from his social setting allows you to incorporate negative reprimand. This type of punishment has unwanted side-effects such as the dog thinking that his master moving towards him is bad.

o Determine what space or area will be designated for time outs. Try to find a spot that isn't intimidating or enjoyable for the dog. Make sure the spot is a safe one. Places to consider include the bathroom (minus the toilet paper), enclosed pantry or gated hallway. If the crate is an acceptable space by the dog, you should utilize it as the time out space.

HE FEELS AFRAID OR SOMEWHAT AGGRESSIVE:

1. Prevent your dog from having a bark fest by avoiding things or places that make him bark. This is a temporary fix for an instant problem, but can help teach the dog that there's nothing to fear. Try this for one week leading up to the training process, which will allow the dog's mind and body to relax.

2. Remain calm.

3. Consult with a professional trainer for individualized sessions.

4. Persuade the dog to calm down about the thing that is upsetting him.

5. Command the dog to concentrate on you by saying "Watch Me".

6. Give treats and praises for him behaving calmly.

Mental and Physical Stimulation for Dogs

Dogs are naturally vibrant and upbeat animals. They vary in size and appearance but are similar in their ability to perceive things and have fun. It is important to participate in activities, games and exercises that encourage mental and physical stimulation for your dog.

Mental Stimulation

Are you seeking ways to keep your dog mentally stimulated? Fortunately, mental stimulation also prompts a routine of healthy living. It does more than sharpen his mind but it also adds enrichment to their lives because stimulation exercises are meaningful and require dedication and attention from your dog. Most owners find that once their dogs embark upon mental stimulation activities they are less bored and spend less time barking or getting into things they shouldn't.

Here are some exercises that work to improve mental stimulation for dogs.

1. No Free Food

   Your dog is living the life. He is not trained to fix his own food but instead just walk up to his bowl and indulge. Not to say it's bad at all but definitely nothing close to the natural abilities they have to scavenge for food. To encourage mental stimulation you can modify his food routine. Instead of adding food to his bowl throughout the day make it fun by playing a little game.

   Use a toy that dispenses food and put his food inside the toy. Once the food is inside the toy, have the dog roll the toy around on the floor in an effort to get the food from the exit hole of the toy. This can get noisy but that adds to the mental stimulation, as it encourages the dog to ignore the noise and focus on working to get his food. Once the first few pieces of food comes out of the toy, your dog will have perceived what's going on and will likely find it quite enjoyable.

2. Sniff and See

    Dogs look forward to daily walks. They possibly see this as one of the biggest joys in life. You can add mental stimulation to the walk by letting your dog sniff more often than usual. While walking is a healthy physical activity, it also gives dogs an opportunity to see things outside the home. Even on the same route each day, dogs will see new things and sniff new smells.

    If you prefer, you can designate the spots and times that he is allowed to sniff. Make sure he is confident and comfortable with the cue for – go sniff – and give him a few minutes to see something different. You may be surprised to see just how tired this makes your dog because he's spent time sniffing and seeing, instead of strictly walking the course.

3. Your Dog Wants a Puzzle

    It may be a toy but it's also a puzzle that mentally stimulates your dog and entertain him as well. Puzzles are interactive tools that work to help dogs focus. They also encourage behaviors that help to solve problems they encounter daily.

    Puzzles are good for dogs because they offer an opportunity for them to activate their natural ability to solve problems. Continuously introducing your dog to toys that are interactive and require them to think is a positive way to enhance their confidence and make them mentally fatigued.

    There are a variety of dog puzzles to choose from. Introduce a few different ones to your dog to see which type he prefers. It's best to offer a variety of them throughout the week so he won't get burned out on playing with just one.

4. Dog Meets Tricks

    Does your dog have any tricks under his paw? Have they mastered the commands of stay, sit and come here? There is so much more that he can learn if you are up to introducing him to a few tricks.

Dogs are mentally stimulated when introduced to a different trick or new command. This is especially beneficial for fearful or timid dogs. The added training will work to improve the confidence of your dog and the bond he has with his owner. Most importantly, learning different tricks enhances his etiquette skills as well.

5. Introduce Nose Games

Most dogs enjoy games that involve the nose. It allows them to find thigs with the nose and is an easy approach to activating their natural sniffing skills. The time spent searching for certain things will lead them to use their brain to think throughout the activity.

You can play games with him that encourage him to 'go get it.' Use a couple small bites of a carrot and put them out of sight. Any treat will work but at first, use a treat that has a scent until the dog figures out how to play the game.

Command him to 'stay' as you hid the treats. If this game is new to you also, use easy hiding spots and commend the dog once he finds the treats. It's fun for the dog if he's praised every time he sniffs out a treat. Once he's caught on to how the game works, make it a little more challenging by putting it in places that he may not think to look, to motivate him to use his nose instead of his eyes to find it.

6. Name That Toy

You know the names of your dog's toys but does he? The 'go get it' is a fun and exciting games for dogs but treats aren't the only item they should be encouraged to "get". You should incorporate a few of his toys into the game also.

In order to be successful at playing this game, the dog would first needs to know the name of his toys. You can begin by sitting alongside your dog and one of his toys. For an example we'll use a stuffed blue fish. Place the blue fish down in front of the dog and say 'blue fish.' Once the dog grabs it or touches the stuffed toy, go overboard with the praises.

Once the game has been done several times with the blue fish, introduce another toy to him by now. Never move forward before the dog clearly understands what the current toy is called. Once he can identify a few of his toys by name, you can take the 'go find it' game to the next level.

7. What To Do With This

Dogs are naturally curious and this mentally stimulating game arouses his curiosity. The objective is to introduce an item such as a box or any safe item to the dog. Place it on the floor and watch as the dog investigates it to determine what he should do with it.

8. Create an Obstacle Course

    It's understandable how an obstacle course or maze is mentally stimulating. With this activity, your dog will learn to complete an obstacle course. You can use poles, bars and agility equipment if you have any, if not just grab whatever you have around the house that would work for an obstacle course.

    If you're not the creative type, use alternative devices to make the course. A few suggestions are blankets, stuffed toys, orange cones and boxes or crates. It doesn't have to look professional but it enables him to learn another trick by completing it.

    Encourage your dog to walk to the blanket, jump over the stick, and maneuver through or around the cones. Implement any commands that work well with the materials in your obstacle course. Creating a nice pattern of obstacles gives them a mental workout. They're not just tasked with one simple thing but multiple things in a row. It's fun and exciting for your dog.

9. Interactive Activities

    Dogs enjoy playing with their owners and interactive activities is a good way to encourage mental stimulation. Play may seem to be a basic activity but it's truly underrated. Research indicates that the more often a dog plays around he has a lesser chance of displaying behavioral problems.

Interactive activities are done by actively playing with or engaging the dog. A simple game of fetch is considered interactive. Games like this are ideal for encouraging mental stimulation. The games are fun and can improve your bond. A game of tug incorporates increased physical play and is great exercise, lots of fun and teaches him good manners.

10. Under the Rock

This game is fun, requires mental thought and doesn't use a rock per say, but the concept is similar. With this game, place a treat under one of two or three containers that are all the same in appearance. The primary objective will be for him to select the container with the treat hidden underneath.

With this game, allow the dog to watch you to see which container you put the treat underneath. Mix them all around and encourage him to find it. Your dog is mentally stimulated and it's a simple method that assists them with problem solving methods.

Do You Really Know Your Fur Baby?

Social media is filled with quizzes and games that encourage users to guess everything from age to what their favorite foods are, or your favorite breed of dog. Many time we participate in quizzes that add no value to life, but they're fun and we're curious creatures.

The same is true about the habits of your dog, or if learning more about their behavior or personality interests you.

Of course each dog has a different personality, but it's a common belief that there are a specific category of personalities that a dog will have.

This is a test that can be done to teach you about the character of your dog.

For anyone that hasn't done this before, a psychometric exam is a method that measures personality traits, examining someone's response to specific scenarios, assessing someone's answers to a particular question which might or might not have a correct or incorrect answer and various forms of testing which works to reveal a basic picture of the nature of someone's personality. This type testing is quite common among testers who wish to find out if someone is a good fit for a certain type of job.

The four categories of personality for dogs are grouped as drives. They include Prey, Pack, Defense (Fight) and Defense (Flight) drive.

All dogs have these type drives but as they age, the levels of the drive change. Owners will experience a better life with ease in the approach to training and the dog is happier when drives are correctly assessed to determine the most prevailing.

In regards to quizzing the dog, you may be led to discover that they're more willing to chew on the test paper rather than answer the questions. Therefore, you must answer on his behalf.

Here are the drives that dogs present:

Prey:

Hunting instincts are overseen by this drive. This drive is typical in dogs that excite easily and love to chase.

Dogs that love the chase and can't resist running after or pursuing things that passes by, regardless of distance. This indicates that the dog has a resilient prey drive. Dogs with an increased prey drive are somewhat more challenging to train. Especially when the owner has almost no experience in training dogs. If you can break down the wall and tap into their energy, dogs of this type can begin to excel in the area of obedience, working challenges and anything that may require large amounts of physical or mental stimulation.

Pack Drive

Every dog is considered a pack type animal. Some types are more accomplished at being in a pack than others. Dogs that have a resilient pack drive are dedicated to their family and the role they play in it. They flourish when the order of the pack is clear. They enjoy and respect their designated role regardless if it's to protect or be protected.

Pack dogs are not interested in activities or anything that disrupts the life of the pack. They are typically calm, adjusts easily to things around them, non-confrontational and easy to please, family type dogs. They will hardly, if at all, need dominating and are eager to do as instructed when it involves maintaining peace among the pack.

Defense (FLIGHT) Drive:

Whenever you encounter a dog that barks aggressively at you and is obviously not pleased with the encounter, if he is an elevated defense drive dog that has the instinct of flight, then it's highly likely that whenever you make confident steps toward him, without aggression but fully assured in yourself, he will probably run away in an effort to get away from you.

If you have not cornered or trapped him into an enclosed space, he will almost always make a run for it. Dogs with this drive are extremely jittery or questionable about new encounters. They are fearful of anything that appears to pose a threat to their space. You can almost anticipate that they'll bark aggressively in panic as they plan their getaway.

If you trap or corner a dog that has a defense (flight) drive, you may be bitten – hard, consistently and quickly. He is biting out of fear for his well-being.

This personality trait may be eliminated by offering nourishment to the dog. Don't confuse aggressive behavior with bold behavior. This type dog needs consistent reassurance and most of all never capitalize on the things they fear. While it's funny to watch a dog scour or jump at the sound of thunder or a loud blender, but doing this constantly to a dog with the Defense (FLIGHT) drive can prove problematic.

Defense (FIGHT) Drive:

The dog that has this drive rarely runs away, jumps on furniture when the blender comes on or other similar occurrences. This dog attacks when they are threatened and doesn't stall or try to escape what they perceive as a threat. Most dogs with this drive has the kill or get killed demeanor in most situations of conflict. They have a naturally dominant stance, often defensive and almost never afraid.

Defense drive animals need a strong owner. It is more difficult to curb a natural attack instinct than to soothe the flight response in confrontational circumstances. Owners of this type dog MUST be a winner. Win the challenges, stand firm on your rules without backing off, even if you lose games that are played, represents a form of weakness in the mind of your dog. This could be an issue as he grows older. Consistency and the ability to read the little indicators of this defense type drive, as well as body language everything will be okay and you shouldn't have much difficulty. Owners must possess a resilient personality, be good leaders and remain consistent in raising this type of dog.

Answer **YES** or **NO** to gain a better perspective of your dog's personality.

SCENARIO	YES	NO
1. Your dog loves food more than he loves you. If you move the food bowl, does he growl?		
2. Your dog sits, but moves around and shakes his head when sitting down.		
3. You have a smart dog but it takes time to train him before he gets it!		
4. Strangers and unfamiliar noises frighten your dog.		
5. Your dog turns over on his back whenever you command him to sit.		
6. Your dog runs from being petted and retreats to a space with his tail tucked.		
7. Your dog consistently jumps on you or others.		

SCENARIO	YES	NO
8. Your dog becomes extremely excited at the sight of you and sometimes wets the floor.		
9. Your dog loves to run circles and get petted and often times ignores other commands when doing so.		
10. You and your dog engage each other in the eyes and understand what is being communicated.		
11. Your dog works hard to please you.		
12. You have to execute commands to prevent your dog from going behind or doing whatever you and your family do.		

Test Results

Your canine could be a single or a mixture of personalities. If a dog has a mixture of personalities, try to identify his most dominant tendency.

Answer Key

- Dominant/Hostile: A YES answer to either of question numbered 1-3

- Compliant/Afraid: A YES answer to either of questions numbered 4-6

- Hyperactive/Easily Excited: A YES answer to either of question numbered 7-9

- Respectful/Receptive: A YES answer to either of question numbered 10-12

Dominant/Hostile Characteristics

If you entered a YES answer to any of questions 1-3, your dog may possibly have a dominant/hostile personality. This type dog may be extremely aggressive or with proper training, a great protector. It's ideal to have this type dog trained by a professional if he has a habit of trying to bite others, growls fiercely, or jumps at people he doesn't know. A dominant type dog is typically quite intelligent and, with quality training will take heed to the leadership and guidance of his owner. They will also make great companions.

Dominant/Hostile Training Strategies

The first priority is to make it clear that you are the leader of the family. Pay attention to any indicators that show that the dog is attempting to take control of situations that you should be controlling and stop it immediately. During training, use a loud clear voice without yelling but your conduct should present firm and without evoking harm.

Compliant/Afraid Characteristics

If you gave a YES answer to at least one of questions 4-6, you may have a submissive or compliant type dog that is shy and somewhat afraid in personality. Although it is important that he obeys your commands and understands his role in the pack, an overly submissive or compliant dog that shivers up whenever you enter a room is not good. Although shyness among dogs is a natural instinct for some, fear or being constantly afraid is sometimes a sign of previous abuse. You can easily train a compliant dog to be warm and welcoming to others and excited to please you, the owner.

Compliant/Afraid Training Strategies

A compliant dog is super sensitive around elevated voice levels or direct eye contact. Hence, try to evade both of these. A quality mixture of gentleness and firm repetition and encouragement will help the dog to gain confidence. It could take longer for a compliant dog to develop trust than other dogs do. When letting them sit alongside you, be gentle about it and make no demands of him until he's comfortable accompanying you while sitting. Once trust is gained, you can slowly start training him the basics. If the dog growls or is difficult to adjust to you, consider professional training.

Hyperactive/Easily Excited

If you gave a YES answer to at least one of questions 7-9, your dog may have a hyperactive personality. This type dog has loads of energy and is always excited and eager to play. This can result in excessive tail-wagging, constant running throughout your home, or sometimes frequently urinating uncontrollably.

Hyperactive/Easily Excited Training Strategies

Dogs in this personality category require a lot of

exercise to deplete their nervous type energy. Brief training periods combined with physical activity and play are more beneficial than extended sessions of training that tire you out while the dog is running on recycled energy that never ends. An overly excited dog requires an owner that is firm and attention-demanding with a captivating voice. The excitement can cause him to wet inside the house often and if so, he needs minimal eye contact and attention upon the owner entering the home. Keep him somewhere to prevent him from easily accessing you the moment you walk through the door. Greet him nicely but neutrally and with an elevated tone. If you sound too excited to see him, he may get overly excited and return to old wetting habits. Once you have been at home for a while, allow him to come over to you, and follow up with a simple praise. You should take him outside immediately to prevent an accident.

Respectful/Receptive

Lastly, if you gave a YES answer to at least one of the final 3 questions, your dog is respectful and receptive to most training techniques. Most often, this type dog is the easiest to train. He gladly accepts and adjusts to the role that he's assigned with the family and strives to make his owner content.

Respectful/Receptive Training Strategies

You should find that a dog that is respectful will respond or be receptive to almost all types of training, especially if you remember to praise him and give celebratory attention for his efforts. A dog with this personality flourishes from training and sees it as an opportunity to show his dedication to his owner. If given consistent, serene voices, and excited type praise, it will likely be the only things required for your dog to learn the simple commands.

Dog Training Guidelines for the Beginner

So you have a new fur baby and are eager to get him trained. The basis or foundation of a good or obedient dog is a quality training technique. While there are really no bad dogs, the same can't be said for owners. They're not bad but lack of knowledge can lead to bad situations.

Typically, dogs will thrive when boundaries or a routines are predictable. When they don't receive quality training, it is not clear to them how they should behave. Dogs are healthier and happier when they are trained and the owner will find that he is easy to be around and teach new things.

The Initial Phases of Training

If your pup is new or you've had him for a while, you should put an effective training plan in place. You should:

- Put together some dog training equipment

- Design a schedule

- Study all available info about training methods that you can apply at home

Six Week Dog Training Program

Whether your dog is young or old, a strategic schedule will help you adhere to the training program. You should experience a rewarding outcome.

Follow the outline of this schedule to help establish good or modify the behavior of your dog.

WEEK 1

- The first week should involve teaching your dog simple commands, such as sit. Designate at least five minutes up to four times per day practicing this command. If the dog isn't trained to use a crate, this is the time to train him. Crates are significant tools that help to manage dogs in the owner's absence. Take some time each day to help him become comfortable using the crate by allowing him to sit inside it for just a few minutes, numerous times throughout the day.

- Develop a routine during the first week because dogs like consistency and routines offer that. Make a schedule for meals, physical activity and walks. It is important to abide by this schedule whenever possible. It is helpful in housetraining and similar other issues also.

- Purchase a few toys for your dog. Choose a variety that includes ones that will offer mental stimulation and excitement. Rotate playtime with the toys to keep it interesting and to give your dog something to look forward to doing each day.

WEEK 2

- Spend several minutes daily with the dog working on the down command and training him the emergency recall order.

- He should have grown accustomed to the crate by now. Try letting him remain in it for more time than you did in the beginning. 2- 3 hours each time will work. Place toys inside the crate. Use it throughout all 6 weeks of training.

- You should begin walking the dog on a loose leash once daily to give him time to practice. Continue this throughout the entire training schedule.

WEEK 3

- This week begin training your dog on "come" and "leave it." Just as the previous weeks, work on the commands a few times daily.

- Teach the dog not to jump on you or others. Set aside a few times each day to focus on this and the other commands. You may choose to wait until it occurs or schedule it for a particular time throughout the day.

- Dedicate 10 minutes to go over all the commands from this and the previous weeks.

WEEK 4

- This week you will work on the command "wait". Incorporate it into your original training or watch for opportunities to present themselves throughout the day and make it a teachable moment.

- Train your dog to walk to a particular area and tell him to lie down. This is ideal to practice during dinner time, when watching television or while reading a book.

WEEK 5

- During this week you can practice the "drop it" training command. Just as you did in previous weeks, spend a few minutes multiple times daily. You can await an opportunity or create one to train in that area.

- Incorporate "quiet" and "speak" into this week's training. You can use this whenever he barks or growls or makes other unwarranted sounds.

Week 6

You've made it to the final week and hopefully, everything has worked well up to this point.

- Select a trick to introduce to the dog now that he's comfortable with the simple commands. You may consider implementing "roll over" and "play dead."

- Dog should be comfortable and familiar with the leash. If you choose to exercise more control while walking him, introduce him to the "heel" command when out for walks.

- Finally, the dog is likely acquainted with several commands and displays quality behaviour. Training isn't over but the basics have been covered. Practice and reinforcement of training moving forward is necessary.

Training does take dedication and a little time and lots of positive reinforcement. The investment is definitely worth it and the result is a happy dog and a happy owner.

Disclaimer

The opinions and ideas of the author contained in this publication are designed to educate the reader in an informative and helpful manner. While we accept that the instructions will not suit every reader, it is only to be expected that the recipes might not gel with everyone. Use the book responsibly and at your own risk. This work with all its contents, does not guarantee correctness, completion, quality or correctness of the provided information. Always check with your medical practitioner should you be unsure whether to follow a low carb eating plan. Misinformation or misprints cannot be completely eliminated. Human error is real!

Picture: dragon_fang // www.shutterstock.com

Design: Olviaprodesign

Printed in Great Britain
by Amazon

33703344R00066